The Mustard Lovers Cookbook

Make Merry with Mustard – Savory Recipes:
Appetizers, Snacks, Sides Mains

BY

Christina Tosch

Copyright 2019 Christina Tosch

Copyright Notes

Table of Contents

Introduction

From Dijon to yellow, spicy to wholegrain, ready- made, powdered or in its seed form, mustard is a versatile kitchen staple.

Not only is mustard a useful condiment but also an ingenious ingredient for all sorts of savory recipes.

The Mustard Lovers' Cookbook will elevate your family meals to a whole new level.

It can add a kick to sauces, flavor to one-pot stews and casseroles, and is the perfect glaze for meat, fish, and more.

Choose from appetizers and snacks, sides and main meals including:

- Creamy Mustard Hummus
- Honey Mustard Ribs
- Tangy Mustard Ribs
- Wicked Deviled Eggs
- Pineapple, Onion and Cabbage Slaw with Honey Mustard
- Sweet Mustard Potato Salad
- Pork Stew with Mustard Seeds
- Sweet Mustard Salmon

If you are searching for new cooking ideas suitable for all occasions then look no further than the Mustard Lovers' Cookbook.

There has never been a better time to Make Merry with Mustard!

Appetizers Snacks

Brie, Bacon and Cranberry Filo Bites

Serve these fresh-from-the-oven ooey-gooey cheesy bites at your next Christmas or New Year's party.

Servings: 24

Total Time: 30mins

Ingredients:

- 2 (19x10") sheets of filo pastry
- 2 ounces unsalted butter (melted)
- 5½ ounces Brie cheese
- 1-2 tsp wholegrain mustard
- 4 ounces cranberry sauce
- 3 ounces smoked back bacon rashers (cut into ½"strips)
- Freshly ground black pepper

Directions:

1. Preheat main oven to 375 degrees F.

2. Take 1 sheet of filo pastry and cover the remaining sheets with a clean damp tea towel; this will prevent it from drying out.

3. Cut the pastry sheet in half.

4. Take 1 half of the filo pastry and lightly brush it with melted butter.

5. Cut into 20 (2") squares.

6. Take 3 of the squares and arrange them one on top of one another. Position each one at a slight angle to the one under it, to create a star shape.

7. Gently push the pastry stack into one of the holes of a 12-cup mini muffin pan. This is to create an empty pastry case.

8. Repeat process with the remaining filo pastry until all 24-cups of the muffin pans are filled.

9. Slice the Brie cheese into 24 evenly sized pieces.

10. Place one piece of cheese into each pastry case.

11. Dot the cheese with a dab of mustard followed by a small dollop of the cranberry sauce.

12. Top with 2-3 strips of bacon.

13. Bake the bites in the oven for 10-12 minutes, until the bacon is sufficiently cooked, the cheese entirely melted and pastry golden.

14. Set aside to cool in the muffin tins for 2-3 minutes, before carefully removing.

15. Serve and enjoy.

Corn Chowder

This is the perfect snack for all you couch potatoes out there. So snuggle up with a great movie and a big bowl of creamy corn chowder, sit back and relax.

Servings: 4

Total Time: 30mins

Ingredients:

- 2 tbsp butter
- 2 tbsp flour
- 2 tsp mustard powder
- 2 cups chicken stock
- 2 cups canned sweet corn (drained)
- 1 (1 pound) small-size ham steak (cut into cubes)
- Salt and pepper
- 1 green onion (peeled, finely chopped)
- ⅔ cup heavy cream

Directions:

1. Melt the butter in a pan over low heat.

2. Add the flour along with the mustard powder to the pan and over low heat, cook while constantly stirring for 1-2 minutes.

3. A little at a time, stir in the stock, and again over moderate heat, bring to boil while continually stirring until thickened.

4. Add the sweet corn along with the ham. Season to taste.

5. Cover with a lid and cook for 5-8 minutes while frequently stirring.

6. Add the green onions along with the heavy cream and continue to cook without boiling.

7. Serve.

Creamy Mustard Hummus

Give extra taste, bite and color to a classic hummus dip with wholegrain Dijon mustard. Serve with healthy crisp veggie batons or warm pita.

Servings: 30-35

Total Time: 20mins

Ingredients:

- 1 (19 ounce) can chickpeas (drained, rinsed)
- 2 tbsp tahini paste
- 3 sprigs of parsley
- ½ tsp cumin
- ½ tsp salt
- 3 garlic cloves (peeled)
- ½ cup olive oil
- 2 tbsp wholegrain Dijon mustard
- Veggie batons or pitta (to serve, optional)

Directions:

1. Add the chickpeas, parsley, tahini paste, salt, cumin, garlic, olive oil, and Dijon mustard to a food processor.

2. On high, process until silky smooth.

3. Transfer to fridge until ready to serve. Transfer to fridge until ready to serve. the hummus can be kept in refrigerator for up to 7 days.

4. Serve with veggie batons or crusty bread.

Crispy Salmon Bites

These salmon nibbles tick all the finger food boxes. They are fast to prepare, and delicious served alongside a green salad or dip.

Servings: 2

Total Time: 15mins

Ingredients:

- 1 (6 ounce) can wild salmon (drained)
- 1 tbsp Dijon mustard
- 2 tbsp mayonnaise
- 1 clove of garlic (peeled, minced)
- 2 tbsp red onion (peeled, minced)
- ½ small-size green pepper (diced)
- ¼ tsp dill
- ⅛ tsp cayenne pepper
- 2 tbsp almond flour
- ½ cup panko breadcrumbs
- Salt and black pepper (to taste)
- Extra virgin oil (to fry)

Directions:

1. Combine all the ingredients (salmon, mustard, mayonnaise, garlic, onion, green pepper, dill, cayenne pepper, almond flour, and breadcrumbs in a mixing bowl. Season with salt and pepper. Mash to incorporate.

2. Form the mixture into small-size patties and transfer to the fridge for 15 minutes.

3. Sprinkle the breadcrumbs onto a shallow dish.

4. Press the crumbs into patties on both sides.

5. Heat a pan to moderate-high heat and drizzle sufficient oil to just coat the pan.

6. In batches, place the patties in the pan. Pan-fry for a couple of minutes on each side, until golden.

7. Transfer to a kitchen paper towel and repeat with the remaining patties, adding oil as necessary.

8. Serve and enjoy with a green salad or favorite dipping sauce.

Dutch Mustard Soup

There are a lot of different mustards available in the Netherlands and many regions have their own types of mustard soup.

Servings: 4

Total Time: 30mins

Ingredients:

- 1 tbsp butter
- 2 onions (peeled, chopped)
- 1 garlic clove (peeled, chopped)
- 3⅓ cups water
- ¾ cup cooking cram
- 1 vegetable bouillon cube
- ½ pound bacon cubes
- 1 leek (cleaned, and thinly sliced)
- 3 tbsp coarse grain mustard
- 1 tbsp cornstarch
- 1 multigrain baguette

Directions:

1. In a deep-sided soup pan, melt the butter.

2. Put onion and garlic to the pan and sauté for 3 minutes.

3. Add the water along with the cooking cream and add the vegetable cube. Bring to boil and allow to boil.

4. In the meantime, in a frying pan, fry the bacon cubes for 8 minutes.

5. Next, add the leek along with the mustard and stir to combine. Allow over low heat, to boil for an additional 4 minutes.

6. Add a splash of water into the cornstarch into a small bowl. Pour the cornstarch mixture into the soup to thicken while stirring.

7. Season with salt and pepper.

8. Serve with multigrain baguette.

Grilled Shrimp with Lime and Brown Mustard Seed Sauce

If this recipe doesn't transport you to the Tropics, then nothing will! Juicy grilled shrimp served with a coconut lime and mustard seed sauce, what's not to like?

Servings: 6-8

Total Time: 25mins

Ingredients:

- 2 tbsp brown mustard seeds
- 3 tbsp fresh cilantro (finely chopped)
- 3 tbsp freshly squeezed lime juice
- 2 tbsp coconut oil (melted, divided)
- ½ tsp coarse sea salt (divided)
- 1½ pounds Jumbo shrimp (shell-on)

Directions:

1. Preheat your grill for moderate-high cooking.

2. Add the mustard seeds to small frying pan and cook, while frequently shaking the pan for 3 minutes, or until the seeds are fragrant and toasted.

3. Allow the seeds to slightly cool, before transferring them to a spice grinder. Crush the seeds.

4. Transfer the seeds to a large-size bowl and stir in the cilantro, lime juice, 1 tablespoon of coconut oil, and ¼ teaspoon of sea salt. Set to one side.

5. In a second bowl, toss the prepared shrimp with the remaining coconut oil and salt.

6. Thread the shrimp onto 6 (12") metals skewers and put them in a grill basket.

7. Grill the shrimp while turning 2-3 times, for 4-5 minutes total, or until sufficiently cooked through.

8. Add the shrimp the bowl containing the sauce and gently toss to evenly coat.

9. Serve hot and enjoy.

Ham and Leek Mini Quiches

A party-pleasing appetizer is always a welcome addition to a buffet, and this no-cutlery needed savory snack is sure to be a big hit.

Servings: 24

Total Time: 30mins

Ingredients:

- 3 sheets frozen ready-rolled shortcrust pastry (partially thawed)
- 2 tsp olive oil
- ½ small leek (trimmed, washed, halved, finely chopped)
- 1¾ ounce shaved leg ham (finely chopped)
- 1 tsp wholegrain mustard
- Salt (to taste)

Egg Mix:

- 4 medium-size eggs
- ¼ cup pure cream
- ¼ cup Parmesan cheese (finely grated)
- Salt and black pepper (to season)

Directions:

1. Preheat the main oven to 350 degrees F.

2. Using a 2¾ "pastry cutter, cut out 24 rounds from the pastry.

3. Press the pastry circles into 2 (12-hole) patty pans of 1½ tablespoon capacity.

4. Over moderate-high heat, heat the oil in a pan.

5. Add the leek to the pan and while occasionally stirring cook until softened for 4 minutes.

6. Remove the pan from the heat and stir in the ham along with the mustard. Set aside to cool. Lightly season with salt.

7. For the egg mix: add the eggs, cream, and grated cheese to a jug. Whisk well to combine.

8. Season with salt and black pepper.

9. Divide the ham mixture between the pastry cases.

10. Brush with the egg mix and bake in the oven until set and golden, for 12-15 minutes.

11. Enjoy.

Honey Mustard Ribs

Ribs are the ultimate appetizer, but this rib recipe featuring a honey mustard glaze elevates this classic dish to an appetizer to remember.

Servings: 4

Total Time: 1hour 40mins

Ingredients:

Ribs:

- One rack baby back ribs (membrane removed)
- Oil (to rub)
- Salt (to rub)
- ⅓ cup French-style honey mustard

Glaze:

- 2 tbsp butter
- ¼ cup runny honey
- 1 tbsp French-style honey mustard
- ½ tbsp cayenne
- ½ tbsp paprika
- 1 tsp garlic powder
- 1 tsp salt

Directions:

1. Preheat the grill to moderate-low heat until it reaches a temperature of 300 degrees F.

2. Arrange the ribs on an aluminum foil-covered baking tray.

3. Rub the ribs all over with oil and salt.

4. Brush the mustard on both sides, covering the ribs.

5. Fold the aluminum foil over the ribs to create an enclosed package. With a knife, poke 2-3 venting slits into the package.

6. Place the foil package on the grill, close the lid and cook for between 1-2 hours or until the ribs are tender but not beginning to fall apart.

7. For the glaze: Over low heat, in a small pan, melt the butter.

8. Add the remaining ingredients (honey, mustard, cayenne, paprika, garlic powder, and salt) and whisk to combine. Allow the glaze to simmer for 2-3 minutes. Remove the pan from the heat.

9. Unwrap the aluminum foil and evenly spread the glaze over the ribs.

10. Oil the grill and increase the heat to high.

11. Grill the ribs on both sides for 10-15 minutes, until caramelized.

12. Remove the ribs from the grill and allow to cool for 8-10 minutes before slicing.

13. Enjoy.

Mussels Steamed in a Dijon Mustard Cream Sauce

Discover what the French have known for a very long time, mussels in white wine and mustard are an appealing and tasty appetizer. Serve with French bread.

Servings: 4

Total Time: 35mins

Ingredients:

- 1 tbsp butter
- 2 shallots (finely sliced)
- 2 garlic cloves (peeled, crushed)
- 2 bay leaves
- 6 sprigs fresh thyme
- ¼ cup white wine
- ½ tsp salt
- ¼ tsp black pepper
- 2 pounds mussels (cleaned)
- 2 tbsp Dijon mustard
- ½ cup half and half
- A small handful of fresh parsley (chopped, to decorate)
- French bread (optional)

Directions:

1. Over moderate-low heat, heat a large deep-sided pot with a tight-fitting lid. Add the butter and melt.

2. Once melted, add the shallots, bay leaves, garlic and sprigs of thyme.

3. Sauté for approximately 5 minutes, until the shallots are softened but not colored.

4. Pour in white wine and season with salt and black pepper. Mix to combine.

5. Cover the pan with a lid and turn the heat to moderate-high.

6. Set the timer for 5 minutes and allow the mixture to come to boil and steam the mussels.

7. Once the mussels are sufficiently cooked, remove them from the pan, and using a slotted spoon, transfer them to a serving platter. Remove and get rid of any mussels that don't open.

8. Return the pan to low heat, whisk in the mustard along with the half and half. Do not allow the sauce to boil.

9. Taste, adjust the seasoning and pour the sauce over the mussels.

10. Remove and discard the bay leaves and freshly thyme.

11. Decorate with fresh parsley and serve with French bread to mop up the sauce.

Whole Grain Mustard Sauce Roasted Shrimp Cocktail

This seafood cocktail is made with seasoned and roasted shrimp and served with a creamy mustard sauce. It is a fabulous festive appetizer too.

Servings: 6-8

Total Time: 20mins

Ingredients:

Shrimp:

- 1 pound shrimp (peeled, deveined)
- 2 tbsp olive oil
- 1 small-size lemon (thinly sliced)
- Salt and freshly ground black pepper

Mustard Sauce:

- ¾ cup full fat mayonnaise
- 2 tbsp shallots (mince)
- 2¼ tbsp wholegrain mustard
- 1 tbsp lemon juice
- 1 tbsp fresh parsley (minced)
- ¼ tsp salt
- ¼ tsp freshly ground black pepper

Directions:

1. Preheat the main oven to 425 digress F.

2. In a bowl, toss the shrimp along with the oil and lemon slices, salt, and black pepper.

3. Transfer the shrimp to a baking sheet and spread out into an even single layer. Roast in the oven for 7-8 minutes, until the shrimp are opaque and pink.

4. In the meantime, prepare the sauce.

5. In a suitable bowl, whisk the mayonnaise with the shallots, mustard, lemon juice, parsley, salt, and black pepper.

6. Taste the sauce and adjust the seasonings.

7. Move to a serving bowl, cover and chill in the fridge until you are ready to serve.

8. Arrange the shrimp and slices of lemon on a platter and serve the mustard sauce on the side.

9. Enjoy.

Stuffed Pretzel Dippers with Cheesy Mustard

Nothing says let's party like a chip and dip and these stuffed pretzel dippers with cheesy mustard go way beyond any regular recipe.

Servings: 8

Total Time: 50mins

Ingredients:

- Nonstick cooking spray
- 1 (13.8) ounce can refrigerated classic pizza crust
- 12 cocktail smoked link sausages (cut in half crosswise)
- ½ cup water
- 3 tsp baking soda
- ¼ tsp kosher salt
- 8 processed cheese (cut into cubes)
- ¼ cup milk
- 2 tsp spicy brown mustard
- 1 tbsp fresh chives (chopped)

Directions:

1. Preheat main oven to 375 degrees F. Put 8 ramekins in the middles of a 9" round pan. Spritz the outer edge of the pan with nonstick cooking spray.

2. Remove the pizza crust dough from the can and unroll to an even thickness (13x8x½").

3. Using a sharp knife or pizza cutter, cut the rectangle into 6x4 rows to yield 24 squares.

4. Top each square with a piece of sausage.

5. Wrap the dough entirely around the sausage to cover, and firmly press the edges to seal. Roll into a ball. Set to one side.

6. Repeat the process for the remaining dough and pieces of sausage.

7. In a 1-cup measuring cup, microwave the water while uncovered, on high heat for 30-60 seconds, until boiling.

8. Add the baking soda, stirring until entirely dissolved.

9. Dip the stuffed balls of dough, one at a time, into the water mixture.

10. Using a slotted spoon, remove from the water and place around the edge of the pan.

11. Sprinkle salt over the dough balls.

12. Bake in the oven for 20-25 minutes, until the pretzels re golden and baked through.

13. In a small-size microwave-safe bowl, add the cubes of cheese. Pour in the milk and while uncovered, microwave on high for 1-2 minutes, stirring halfway through the microwave time until the cheese is melted.

14. Stir in the brown mustard.

15. Transfer the dip to a bowl and serve with pretzels.

16. Garnish with chopped chives and serve.

Tangy Mustard Wings

Juicy chicken wings in a hot and tangy mustard sauce are great for sharing.

Servings: 2

Total Time: 11hours 45mins

Ingredients:

- 10-12 chicken wings (cut in half at joints, wing tips removed and discarded)
- ½ cup butter
- 2 cups apple cider vinegar
- 4 cups yellow mustard
- 2 tsp onion powder
- 2-3 dashes of hot pepper sauce
- Salt and black pepper

Directions:

1. First, prepare the chicken wings by cutting them in half at the joints, and removing and discarding their wing tips.

2. In a pan over moderate heat, melt the butter.

3. Stir in the vinegar, mustard, onion powder, pepper sauce, salt, and black pepper.

4. Turn the heat down to moderate-low and while stirring simmer until thickened for 5-6 minutes. Cover the sauce and transfer it to the fridge overnight.

5. Preheat the main oven to 350 degrees F.

6. Cover a baking pan with aluminum foil and spray the foil with nonstick spray.

7. Arrange the wigs on the baking pan and bake in the oven for 20 minutes.

8. Remove the chicken wing from the baking pan, allowing any juice to drain away. Put the wings in a slow cooker and add the sauce and toss to coat evenly.

9. On low heat cook for 3-4 hours.

Welsh Rarebit

Turn the Celts' favorite comfort food into appetizer or snack.

Servings: 6-12

Total Time: 15mins

Ingredients:

- 12 ounces sharp Cheddar (grated, divided)
- 1 large-size egg (lightly beaten)
- 2 tbsp stout
- 1 tsp Worcestershire sauce
- 1 tsp English mustard
- Pinch of cayenne pepper
- 12 slices thick white bread

Directions:

1. Set 1 tablespoon of Cheddar cheese to one side.

2. Mix the remaining cheese with the egg, stout, Worcestershire sauce, English mustard, and a pinch of cayenne pepper.

3. Preheat your grill to high and toast the slices of bread on both sides.

4. Spread the cheese mixture evenly over the top and scatter with the cheese set aside earlier.

5. Grill until the cheese entirely melts.

6. Serve and enjoy.

Wicked Deviled Eggs

Put the devil in this egg dish with spicy prepared mustard and enjoy this classic appetizer with a tangy twist.

Servings: 12

Total Time: 20mins

Ingredients:

- 6 large-size hard-boiled eggs (shelled)
- ¼ cup mayonnaise
- 1 tbsp onions (peeled, grated)
- 2 tbsp ready-made mustard
- Salt and black pepper (to season)
- Paprika (to garnish)

Directions:

1. Cut the hard-boiled eggs lengthwise in half.

2. Scoop the yolks out and put them in a bowl.

3. With a fork, mash the yolks and add the mayonnaise, onions, and prepared mustard, mix thoroughly to combine.

4. Season with salt and black pepper. Add additional mustard if needed.

5. Evenly divide the filling and pile it into the egg halves.

6. Garnish with paprika.

7. Cover, chill in the fridge until you are ready to serve.

Sides

Brussels Sprouts and Carrots in Candied Orange Sauce

Crisp Brussels sprouts and bite-tender carrots tossed in a sweet candied orange sauce will have everyone coming back for more.

Servings: 6

Total Time: 20mins

Ingredients

- 3½ cups fresh baby carrots
- 1 pound frozen Brussels sprouts
- 2 tbsp butter
- 2 tbsp freshly squeezed orange juice
- 1 tbsp pure maple syrup
- 1 tbsp Dijon mustard
- ½ tsp orange peel (grated)
- ¼ cup dried cranberries
- 2 tbsp toasted pecans (chopped)

Directions:

1. Cook the carrots until bite-tender.

2. Cook the frozen sprouts according to the package instructions, and until crisp.

3. Drain the veggies and combine the sprouts with the carrots and keep warm.

4. Over moderate-low heat, in a pan melt the butter.

5. Stir in the fresh orange juice, maple syrup, Dijon mustard, and grated peel.

6. Next, add the cranberries and mixed veggies.

7. Toss to evenly coat and serve, garnished with pecans.

Crisp Honey Mustard Parsnips

Add some sweet heat to these parsnips and serve at your next family get-together alongside a home-cooked roast dinner.

Servings: 8

Total Time: 55mins

Ingredients:

- 2 pounds parsnips (peeled, cut into thumb width batons)
- 2 tsp English mustard powder
- 2 tbsp plain flour
- Salt and black pepper (to season)
- 4 tbsp rapeseed oil
- 3 tsp clear runny honey
- Sea salt (to garnish)

Directions:

1. Boil the parsnips for approximately 5 minutes. Drain and set aside to steam dry for 3 minutes.

2. In a bowl, combine the mustard powder with the flour along with a liberal amount of seasoning.

3. Toss the parsnips in the seasoned flour, shaking off any excess.

4. Preheat the main oven 425 degrees F.

5. Pour the rapeseed oil into 2 nonstick baking trays.

6. Heat the oil for 5 minutes in the oven.

7. Carefully add the parsnips to the oil, in a single layer without overcrowding. Turn the parsnips a few times before roasting for half an hour, until crisp and golden.

8. Drizzle the clear honey over the hot parsnips, give them a gentle shake.

9. Garnish with seas salt and serve.

English Mustard Sauce

Enjoy this creamy English mustard sauce as a side with roast meats, fish or salad.

Servings: 6

Total Time: 15mins

Ingredients:

- 2 shallots (finely chopped)
- ½ cup white wine
- 1 bay leaf
- 2 tsp light soft brown sugar
- 2 tbsp English style mustard
- 1 tbsp wholegrain mustard
- 1 cup crème fraiche

Directions:

1. In a pan over moderate heat, combine the shallots with the white wine, bay leaf, and sugar.

2. Simmer until the shallots have softened, and the white wine has reduced by half.

3. Stir in the English mustard along with the wholegrain mustard and crème fraiche.

4. Serve either warm or cold.

Green Beans with Mustard, Mint, and Lemon

Green beans served in a zesty and refreshing vinaigrette is an ideal side for serving with lots of different meats and fish.

Servings: 6

Total Time: 20mins

Ingredients:

- 14 ounces green beans (trimmed)
- 2 tbsp butter
- Freshly squeezed juice of 1 lemon
- Zest of 1 lemon
- 1 tbsp Dijon mustard
- Salt and black pepper
- 3 tbsp mint (chopped)

Directions:

1. Bring a pan of water to boil.

2. Add beans to the pan and cook until bite-tender, for 5-6 minutes. Drain and refresh under cold running water. Put to one side.

3. When you wish to serve, in a pan, melt the butter. Add the lemon juice and zest, mustard, a pinch of salt and a liberal amount of black pepper.

4. Add the green beans and gently toss until well coated.

5. Transfer to a dish, and garnish with chopped mint.

6. Serve your beans with a light vinaigrette of citrus and herbs- they'll match with vegetarian, fish and meat main courses alike.

Hazelnut and Mustard Carrots

Give those Christmas carrots a festive makeover with this mustard and sherry dressing.

Servings: 6-8

Total Time: 20mins

Ingredients:

- 5⅓ tbsp blanched hazelnuts
- 2 tsp Dijon mustard
- 1 tsp red wine vinegar
- 2 tbsp dry sherry
- ¼ cup vegetable oil
- Salt and black pepper
- 17½ ounces carrots (thinly sliced)

Directions:

1. In a dry, non-stick frying pan, toast nuts until golden. Set aside to cool before coarsely chopping or crushing with a pestle and mortar.

2. Whisk the mustard along with the vinegar and dry sherry.

3. Gradually pour in the vegetable oil while continually whisking.

4. Season and put to one side.

5. Boil the carrots for 3-5 minutes, or until bite tender. Drain the carrots and return them to the pan.

6. Pour the dressing over the top, stirring to coat. And over low heat, cook for 1-2 minutes.

7. Garnish with hazelnuts and serve.

Mustard Pickle

This perfect chunky pickle is delicious served with cold cuts of meat, salad, and baby buttered potatoes.

Servings: 16-20

Total Time: 1day 45mins*

Ingredients:

- 8 ounces table salt
- 4 quarts water
- 16 ounces baby onions
- 8 ounces cherry tomatoes
- 16 ounces cauliflower florets
- 16 ounces cucumber (seeded, diced)
- 1 tbsp capers
- 4½ ounces butter
- 1 ounce plain flour
- 17 ounces malt vinegar
- 3½ ounces caster sugar
- 1 tbsp turmeric
- 2½ tsp mustard powder
- Black pepper

Directions:

1. First, dissolve the table salt in the water.

2. Add the onions along with the tomatoes and cauliflower to a large-size bowl and cover with the salty water. Cover with plastic wrap and chill in the refrigerator for 24 hours.

3. Using a colander, was the baby onions, tomatoes, and cauliflower florets and transfer them to a flameproof casserole dish.

4. Add the cucumber followed by the capers and cover with 2 quarts of fresh water. Bring to boil and cook for approximately10 minutes. Drain the veggies and transfer to a large mixing bowl.

5. In a pan, melt the butter.

6. Next, add the flour and stir to make a roux.

7. Gradually and slowly add the vinegar while continually stirring and cook for 3 minutes, until thickened.

8. Add the sugar, turmeric, and mustard powder. Season with pepper.

9. Fill over the veggies and stir well to incorporate.

10. Pack the veggies into a sterilized jar and securely seal.

11. Leave in the refrigerator for a minimum of 5 days before serving. This will help the veggies to absorb all the flavor from the mustard.

12. You can store the pickle in the fridge for up to 6 weeks.

*Plus 5 days pickling time

Mustard Potato Wedges

Mustard is the secret ingredient to this crisp golden fries. Serve with burgers, grilled meats or hotdog and enjoy.

Servings: 4

Total Time: 1hour 5mins

Ingredients:

- 4 medium-size Yukon gold potatoes
- Nonstick cooking spray
- 6 whole shallots (peeled)
- 3 tbsp olive oil
- 2 tbsp mustard
- 1 tsp whole cumin seeds
- 1 tsp salt

Directions:

1. Preheat main oven to 425 degrees f.

2. Cut half of the potatoes and then again in half lengthwise to create 16 wedges.

3. Lightly spritz a roasting pan with nonstick cooking spray.

4. Toss the potato wedges with the shallots, oil, mustard, cumin seeds, and salt in a large-size bowl.

5. In a single layer, spread the potatoes in the pan, placing the potato wedges cut side facing downward.

6. Roast in the oven until golden and crisp for 15-20 minutes.

7. Using a metal spatula, flip the wedges over and roast for an additional 10-15 minutes until crisp and tender on the other side.

8. Serve and enjoy.

Mustard Yorkies

Fluffy golden Yorkshire puddings are a British comfort food to serve alongside a roast dinner. Here, this classic side gets a kick thanks to the addition of wholegrain mustard.

Servings: 12

Total Time:

Ingredients:

- 12 tsp sunflower oil
- 5 ounces plain flour
- Salt and black pepper
- 3 large-size eggs
- 1¼ cups milk
- 1 tbsp wholegrain mustard

Directions:

1. Preheat main oven to 425 degrees F.

2. Add 1 teaspoon of oil into each well of a 12-cup muffin tin and heat in the preheated oven for 5 minutes.

3. In the meantime, mix the flour with a little salt and pepper in a large bowl.

4. Beat the eggs along with milk and wholegrain mustard.

5. Gradually beat into the flour mixture to create smooth batter.

6. Spoon the batter in to the muffin tin.

7. Bake in oven until golden and risen, for 25-30 minutes. Avoid opening the door during the baking time.

8. Invert from the muffin tins and serve.

Pineapple, Onion and Cabbage Slaw with Honey Mustard

This cabbage slaw is a winning combination of fresh juicy fruit and crunchy veg. Swopping regular mayo for mustard gives the dressing a tangy and spicy kick. Serve with grilled chicken or fresh fish.

Servings: 4

Total Time: 15mins

Ingredients:

Dressing:

- 2 tbsp American mustard sauce
- 1 tsp honey
- Freshly squeezed juice of 1 lemon
- 3 tbsp fresh cream
- Salt (to taste)

Slaw:

- 1 cup cabbage (shredded)
- 1 cup pineapple (chopped)
- 1 onion (peeled, sliced)

Directions:

1. First, prepare the dressing. In a large bowl, combine the mustard with the honey, lemon juice, fresh cream and salt, and whip until entirely combined.

2. Add the shredded cabbage along with the pineapple and onion and mix thoroughly.

3. Toss the slaw until the dressing coats the fruit and veggies. Taste and season to your preference.

4. Serve and enjoy.

Roasted Cauliflower in Dijon Mustard Butter-Lemon Sauce

Roasted cauliflower in the oven and served with a buttery lemon and mustard sauce

Servings: 2-4

Total Time: 45mins

Ingredients:

- 1 head of cauliflower (cut into florets)
- 1 tbsp olive oil
- 1 tsp salt
- 6 tbsp butter
- 2 tbsp Dijon mustard
- Freshly squeezed juice of 1 lemon
- Grated rind of 1 lemon
- 1 tbsp fresh parsley (chopped)

Directions:

1. Preheat main oven to 400 degrees F.

2. Arrange cauliflower florets on a baking sheet and drizzle with oil.

3. Season with salt and roast in the oven for just over 20 minutes.

4. Remove the cauliflower from the baking sheet and transfer to an ovenproof casserole dish.

5. In a pan, melt the butter and add the mustard along with the lemon juice and grated lemon rind.

6. Spoon mustard sauce over cauliflower and return to the oven for approximately 10 minutes.

7. Garnish with chopped parsley and enjoy.

Slow Cooker Brown Sugar with Mustard Baked Beans

Super satisfying, these sweet, slow-cooked baked beans are packed full of flavor and texture.

Servings: 12

Total Time: 30hours 10mins

Ingredients:

- 1 pound dry navy beans
- 1 pound thickly-cut bacon (cut into 1" pieces)
- 1 small-size yellow onion (peeled, diced)
- 2 garlic cloves (peeled, finely minced)
- 12 ounces root beer
- 1 cup store-bought BBQ sauce
- ¾ cup brown sugar
- ⅓ cup ketchup
- ¼ cup honey
- ¼ cup yellow mustard
- ¼ cup apple cider vinegar
- 2 tbsp pure maple syrup

Directions:

1. Add the navy beans to a large-size bowl and cover with sufficient water to submerge.

2. Cover the bowl and allow beans to soak overnight.

3. The following day, drain the navy beans and transfer them to a large pan.

4. Once again, submerge in water and over high heat, bring to a rolling boil.

5. Turn the heat down to simmer and cook for 45 minutes. Drain well and put aside.

6. To a large frying pan, add the bacon and over moderate heat cook for 8-10 minutes until crisp.

7. Remove the pan from the heat source and transfer the bacon to a plate lined with kitchen paper towel. Leave the bacon fat remaining the pan.

8. Set the pan over moderate heat and add the onion. Cook the onion for 5-6 minutes, until tender. Add the garlic and cook until fragrant, for 60 seconds or so.

9. To a slow cooker, add root beer along with the BBQ sauce, brown sugar, ketchup, honey, yellow mustard, vinegar, and maple syrup, and whisk well until entirely combined.

10. Next, add the beans, bacon, and onion-garlic mixture to the slow cooker and stir well to coat evenly.

11. On low heat, cook the beans for 8-10 hours, until fork-tender and thickened.

12. Serve at once or, alternatively, transfer to the fridge for 12 hours. This will allow the beans to thicken.

13. Enjoy.

Sweet Mustard Potato Salad

This sweet and tangy potato salad will be more than welcome at your next get-together or cookout.

Servings: 10

Total Time: 20mins

Ingredients:

- 2½ pounds waxy potatoes (cut into small-size chunks)
- 14 ounces mayonnaise
- 2 tbsp American mustard
- 2 tbsp cider vinegar
- 2 tbsp honey
- 4 large-size hard-boiled eggs (peeled, finely chopped)
- Salt and black pepper (to season)
- 8 spring onions (finely chopped)

Directions:

1. Bring the potatoes to boil in a pan of salted water. Cover with a lid and simmer until cooked through, for 8-10 minutes. Drain and leave in the colander to cool.

2. In a bowl, combine the mayonnaise with the American mustard, cider vinegar, honey, and hard-boiled eggs. Season well.

3. Stir the mayonnaise mixture into the potatoes along with half of the spring onions.

4. Transfer to a serving bowl and garnish with the remaining spring onions.

5. Chill in the fridge until you are ready to serve.

Mains

Asian Fish Curry

A fish curry makes a welcome change from any take-out you can buy. It's a lot healthier too and has lots of great spices.

Servings: 4-6

Total Time: 45mins

Ingredients:

- 4 (4 ounce) pieces carp (washed, patted dry)
- 1 tsp garam masala powder
- 1 tsp powdered coriander
- ½ tsp ground turmeric
- 1 tsp red chili pepper
- Salt (to season)
- 3 tbsp fish oil (divided)
- 1 tsp fenugreek seeds
- 2 tsp mustard seeds
- 2 garlic cloves (peeled)
- 2 black cardamom pods
- 1 onion (peeled)
- Water (as needed)
- 1 tsp fresh lime juice (to garnish)
- 1 green chili (chopped, to serve)

Directions:

1. Prepare the fish as directed.

2. In a bowl, combine the garam masala with the coriander, turmeric and red chili powder. Season with salt.

3. Add the fish to the bowl, make sure the fish is coated in the marinade, and put it to one side.

4. Over moderate heat, heat a pan. Add some of the oil to the pan.

5. Remove the fish from marinade, shaking off any excess and fry in the oil until well cooked and browned on both sides.

6. Once cooked, transfer the fish to a large-size bowl.

7. In a grinder, combine the fenugreek seeds with the mustard seeds, garlic cloves, and black cardamoms. Grind to create a smooth paste and set it to one side.

8. Add oil to a second pan and over moderate heat, add the ground paste, and chopped onions, and sauté.

9. Add a drop of water to pan, followed by the fried pieces of fish and simmer over moderate heat for 3-4 minutes.

10. Add a squeeze of fresh lemon juice and chopped chili to serve

Beef and Mustard Pie with Green Beans

Nothing beats a homemade beef pie with buttery puff pastry flavored with wholegrain mustard.

Servings: 4-6

Total Time: 2hours 55mins

Ingredients:

- 2 pounds 2 ounces beef skirt (cut into large-size chunks)
- 2 tbsp plain flour
- Salt and black pepper
- 2 tbsp rapeseed oil
- 7 ounces red wine
- 14 ounces beef stock
- 1 onion (peeled, finely sliced)
- 2 large-size carrots (cut into 1" pieces)
- 3 thyme sprigs
- 2 tbsp wholegrain mustard
- Sea salt and black pepper
- 2 egg yolks (beaten)
- 14 ounces all-butter puff pastry (rolled into ¼" thickness)

Green Beans:

- 10 ounces fine green bans
- 1 ounce butter
- Sea salt and black pepper

Directions:

1. Preheat the main oven to 300 degrees f.

2. In a bowl, toss the beef with the flour and season with salt and black pepper.

3. Heat a large-size baking dish until hot. Add 1 tablespoon of rapeseed oil and sufficient beef to cover the bottom of the dish.

4. Fry the meat until browned, on both sides before removing and put to one side. Repeat with the remaining rapeseed oil and beef.

5. Return the meat to the pan. Pour in the wine and cook until the volume of the liquid is reduced by half before adding the beef stock, onion, carrots, thyme, and wholegrain mustard. Season liberally with salt and black pepper.

6. Cover with a lid and place in the preheated oven for 2 hours.

7. Remove from the oven and taste before adjusting the seasoning. Set to one side to cool. Remove and discard the thyme.

8. Once the meat is sufficiently cooled, assemble the pie.

9. Preheat the main oven to 400 degrees F.

10. Transfer the beef to a casserole dish. Brush the rim with the egg yolks and lay the pastry over the top. Brush the surface of the pie with the beaten yolk.

11. Trim the pastry, leaving enough excess to crimp the edges.

12. Place the pie in the oven and bake for half an hour, until the pastry is golden and the filling cooked through.

13. To prepare the green beans, bring a pan of salted water to boil.

14. Add the green beans to the water and cook until fork-tender, for 4-5 minutes.

15. Drain the beans and toss them with the butter. Season with pepper.

16. Serve the pie alongside the green beans.

Grilled Mustard-Brown Sugar Chicken

Chicken lovers everywhere will really appreciate this sweet and savory poultry main.

Servings: 8

Total Time: 20mins

Ingredients

- ½ cup yellow or Dijon mustard
- ½ tsp ground allspice
- ⅓ cup packed brown sugar
- ¼ tsp crushed red pepper flakes
- 8 (4 ounce) boneless skinless chicken thighs

Directions:

1. In a large bowl, combine the mustard with the allspice, sugar, and red pepper flakes.

2. Remove ¼ cup of the mixture for serving.

3. Add the chicken to remaining mixture and toss to coat.

4. Grill the chicken, covered, over moderate heat for 6-8 minutes on each side.

5. Serve with the mustard mixture set aside earlier.

Honey Mustard, Apple Chicken Sausage

Mustard with a sweet hint of honey and apple jelly brings a lot to this simple chicken sausage dish to enjoy with rice.

Servings: 4

Total Time: 20mins

Ingredients:

- ¼ cup honey mustard
- 2 tbsp apple jelly
- 1 tbsp water
- 1 tbsp olive oil
- 2 medium-size apples (cored, sliced)
- 1 (12 ounce) package fully-cooked chicken sausage links (sliced)
- Rice (hot, cooked)

Directions:

1. In a small-size bowl, whisk the honey mustard with the apple jelly and water until well blended.

2. In a large-size frying pan, heat the oil over moderate heat.

3. Add the slices of apple and cook while stirring until tender, for 2-3 minutes.

4. Remove from the pan

5. Add the sausage to the frying pan and cook while stirring for 2-4 minutes, until browned.

6. Return the apples to the pan, add the mustard mixture and cook while stirring for 1-2 minutes to thicken.

7. Serve with hot, cooked rice.

Lamb, Black Pudding, and Mustard Hotpot

Traditional hotpot gets a modern makeover with black pudding and mustard.

Servings: 4

Total Time: 2hours 35mins

Ingredients:

- 2 tbsp sunflower oil
- 2 large-size onions (peeled, thinly sliced)
- 12¼ ounces black pudding (thickly sliced)
- 8 middle neck lamb chop cutlets (fat trimmed)
- 2 pound potatoes (peeled, very thinly sliced)
- 3 carrots (thinly sliced)
- 2 tbsp grainy mustard
- Salt and black pepper
- A handful of parsley (finely chopped)
- 6 thyme sprigs (leaves only)
- 1¼ pints hot lamb stock
- Knob of butter (melted)

Directions:

1. Preheat the main oven to 355 degrees F.

2. Heat 1 tablespoon of the oil in a frying pan.

3. Add the onions to the pan and cook until they are softened and just beginning to brown for 5 minutes.

4. Remove and put to one side.

5. Pour the remaining tablespoon of oil into the pan and fry the black pudding for 60 seconds on each side. Remove and drain on kitchen paper towel and put to one side.

6. Over high heat, in the pan, cook the lamb chops until the outside is a good color but not cooked through. Drain off any fat and put the lamb chops to one side.

7. Layer the ingredients in a deep ovenproof baking dish. The ingredients should be snug inside the dish. Begin with the slices of potatoes and carrots. Dot half the mustard over each layer of the black pudding and season well in between the layers. You will also need to sprinkle the parsley and thyme leaves between each layer as you do. You will eventually have 2 layers of lamb chops and a final layer of potatoes.

8. Pour the lamb stock over the top and brush with melted butter.

9. Cover the dish and bake in the preheated oven for 2 hours, until the ingredients are tender. Remove the lid for the final 30 minutes to crisp up the slices of potatoes.

Lamb Shanks Braised with Mint and Mustard

Tender fall off the bone lamb, braised in a white wine sauce with the flavor of fresh mint and the heat of the mustard is ideal for any get-together or special occasion.

Servings: 4

Total Time: 2hours 15mins

Ingredients:

- 2 tbsp olive oil
- 4 lamb shanks
- Kosher salt and black pepper
- 3 tbsp shallots (minced)
- 1 garlic clove (peeled and minced)
- 1 cup dry white wine
- 2 cups low-salt chicken broth
- 2 tbsp Worcestershire sauce
- 2 tbsp wholegrain mustard
- Bunch of fresh mint

Directions:

1. Preheat the main oven to 350 degrees F.

2. In a Dutch oven, heat the oil over high heat until it starts to smoke.

3. Season the lamb with salt and black pepper and sear for 4 minutes on each side.

4. Add the shallots along with the garlic, stir until for 15 seconds, until fragrant.

5. Pour in the wine and boil for 60 seconds.

6. Next, add the chicken broth followed by the Worcestershire sauce and wholegrain mustard.

7. Using a wooden spatula, scrape up any browned bits from the base of the pan.

8. Scatter the mint over the top and cover the Dutch oven.

9. Place in the preheated oven and cook for 2-2½ hours until the meat falls easily off the bone.

10. Using kitchen tongs, remove the shanks from the Dutch oven and put on a platter.

11. On the stovetop, simmer the sauce until it reduces to yield 1½ cups. Skim off any surface fat.

12. Season with salt and black pepper and serve.

Mustard and Orange Lamb Chops

Don't hold back on the mustard! The citrus flavors of orange zest combine with the strong flavor of Dijon mustard to brush over juicy lamb chops.

Servings: 4-6

Total Time: 20mins

Ingredients:

- 3 tbsp orange zest (finely grated)
- 1 garlic clove (peeled, crushed)
- 2 tbsp fresh thyme leaves (finely chopped)
- ½ cup Dijon mustard
- 3 tsp dark brown sugar
- 1 tbsp olive oil
- 12 small-size lamb loin chops (excess fat trimmed)
- Salt and black pepper

Directions:

1. In a bowl, combine the orange zest with the garlic and thyme to create a paste.

2. Stir in the mustard, brown sugar, and oil to combine.

3. Preheat the grill.

4. Brush approximately half of the mixture onto each side of the lamb chops and grill for approximately 2 minutes on each side.

5. Turn the chops over and brush the remaining half of the mixture over the lamb chops.

6. Continue to cook until done.

7. Season the chops and serve.

Mustard Fried Catfish

Catfish with a mustard coating and deep-fried until crisp makes a great midweek meal.

Servings: 4

Total Time: 20mins

Ingredients:

- ⅔ cup yellow cornmeal
- ⅓ cup all-purpose flour
- ½ tsp salt
- ¼ tsp paprika
- ¼ tsp pepper
- ⅛ tsp cayenne pepper
- ½ cup prepared mustard
- 4 (6 ounce) catfish fillets
- Oil (to fry)

Directions:

1. In a bowl, combine the cornmeal with the flour, salt, paprika, pepper, and cayenne.

2. Spread mustard over both sides of the catfish and coat with the cornmeal-cayenne mixture.

3. Heat the oil in a deep-fat fryer to 375 degrees F.

4. Fry the fish on each side for 2-3 minutes, until the fish flakes easily when using a ford.

5. Drain on kitchen paper towels.

One-Pot Chickpea and Fall Vegetable Tagine

A tagine is the ideal one-pot meal for the winter months. Serve with couscous and enjoy a taste of North Africa.

Servings: 4-6

Total Time: 55mins

Ingredients:

- 3 tbsp olive oil
- 1 large onion (peeled)
- 2 garlic cloves (peeled, finely chopped)
- 2 cups canned chickpeas
- 1 sweet potato (chopped)
- 2 carrots (sliced)
- 1 cup winter squash (chopped)
- 1 cup packed spinach (finely chopped)
- 1 (14 ounce) can whole tomatoes plus juices (coarsely chopped)
- 1 preserved lemon (diced, including rind)
- ½ cup green olives (roughly chopped)
- 1 tbsp curry powder
- 1 tbsp Rogan Josh seasoning
- 2 tbsp harissa (to taste)
- Couscous (to serve)

Directions:

1. Preheat the main oven to 375 degrees F.

2. Heat approximately 3 tablespoons of olive oil in a Dutch oven or preferably tagine.

3. Add the chopped onions and sauté until translucent. Add the garlic and sauté for 60 seconds.

4. Add the remaining ingredients (chickpeas, sweet potatoes, carrots, winter squash, spinach, tomatoes, diced lemon and rind, olives, curry powder, Rogan Josh, and harissa (to taste). Gently stir to combine. Cover with a lid and cook until the veggies are tender, for about 45 minutes.

5. Taste and season with salt.

6. Serve with couscous and enjoy.

Pasta with Sausage, Basil and Mustard

Go beyond the burgers and dogs. Add mustard to a tasty pasta dish and include it in a sauce.

Servings: 4

Total Time: 20mins

Ingredients:

- 16 ounces penne pasta
- 1 tbsp extra-virgin olive oil
- 8 hot Italian sausages (casings removed, crumbled)
- ¾ cup dry white wine
- ¾ cup heavy cream
- 3 tbsp grainy mustard
- Pinch of crushed red pepper
- 1 cup basil (thinly sliced)

Directions:

1. In a large pot of boiling salty water, cook the pasta until al dente. Drain.

2. In the meantime, heat the oil in a large frying pan.

3. Add the Italian sausage meat and over medium-high heat, brown for 5 minutes.

4. Pour in the dry white wine and simmer, while scraping up the browned bits, until it reduces by half for approximately 5 minutes.

5. Pour in the cream and add the mustard along with the crushed red pepper. Simmer for a couple of minutes.

6. Remove from the heat, and add the drained pasta, toss to evenly coat.

7. Garnish with basil, serve and enjoy.

Pork Stew with Mustard Seeds

This stew will warm you inside and out. Pair it with crusty bread and mop up all those great juices.

Servings: 4

Total Time: 2hours

Ingredients:

- 2 tbsp of olive oil
- 2 yellow onions (peeled, finely chopped)
- 2 cloves garlic (peeled, finely chopped)
- 4 sides of pork spine (total weight 1 pound, cut into cubes)
- ½ cup white wine
- 1½ tbsp brown mustard seeds
- 1¼ cups chicken stock
- 1 tbsp thick cream
- Salt and black pepper

Directions:

1. In a crockpot, warm some olive oil.

2. Add the onion and garlic to the crockpot, and sauté until the onions are translucent.

3. Stir in the cubes of meat and stir-fry for 5-6 minutes, over high heat.

4. Pour in the white wine and allow to reduce by 30 percent.

5. Next, add the mustard seeds, mix to combine, and add the stock.

6. Bring to boil, cover with a lid and turn the heat down under the pot. Simmer until the meat is tender, for 90 minutes.

7. After approximately 90 minutes, the meat should be tender.

8. Stir in the cream and mix to combine.

9. Heat the mixture once more and remove the pan, and once it boils again, remove from the heat. Take care the cream does not boil.

10. Serve with rice or pasta and pour the mustard sauce over the top.

Pork Burgers with Feta Mustard

Spice up a burger with cheesy mustard and enjoy. Feta cheese is the ideal ingredient to combine with whole grain mustard due to its salty flavor and creamy texture.

Servings: 6

Total Time: 30mins

Ingredients:

- ½ tsp garlic powder
- ½ tsp ground coriander
- ½ tsp ground fennel seeds
- ½ tsp paprika
- Salt and black pepper
- 2 pounds ground pork
- 6 hamburger buns (split)
- ¼ cup butter (softened)
- 1 (16 ounce) jar pickled beets (to serve)

Feta Mustard:

- 4 ounces feta cheese (crumbled)
- 3 tbsp mayonnaise
- 3 tbsp wholegrain mustard

Directions:

1. In a bowl, combine the garlic powder with the coriander, fennel, paprika, 1 teaspoon of salt and ½ teaspoon of black pepper. Mix to incorporate.

2. Add the ground pork and mix until the spice blend until evenly combined.

3. Using clean hands, form the mixture into 6 (½" thick) patties.

4. Preheat a large frying pan over moderate-high heat.

5. In batches, fry the patties and cook on each side for 3-5 minutes, or until a meat thermometer registers 145 degrees F.

6. While the burgers cook, in a bowl, combine the feta cheese with the mayonnaise, ad wholegrain mustard, and mix to incorporate. Drain 2-3 (per person) of the pickled beet slices.

7. Put the burgers on a plate and loosely tent with aluminum foil to keep warm.

8. Spread the cut sides of the hamburger buns with butter and toast under the grill until golden.

9. To assemble: Spread the bottom of each split toasted bun with the feta mustard.

10. Top with a pork burger and a few pickled beet slices.

Spicy Mustard Turkey Pizza

Are you short on ideas of what to do with your leftover turkey? No worries, this pizza will solve all your problems.

Servings: 6

Total Time: 15mins

Ingredients:

- 1 (12") store-bought prebaked thin-crust pizza
- 3 tbsp low-fat mayonnaise
- 3 tbsp runny honey
- 3 tbsp spicy brown mustard
- ½ tsp garlic powder
- 2 cups cooked, leftover turkey (cubed)
- 1 cup fresh mushrooms (sliced)
- 5 cooked bacon strips (chopped)
- 1 cup Swiss cheese (shredded)

Directions:

1. Place the crust on a 12" pizza pan.

2. In a bowl, combine the mayo with the runny honey, spicy brown mustard, and garlic powder. Add the leftover turkey to the bowl and toss to coat. Spread the mixture over the crust.

3. Top the pizza with sliced mushrooms, chopped bacon, and Swiss cheese.

4. Bake in the oven at 450 degrees F for 8-12 minutes, until the cheese is entirely melted.

Sweet Mustard Salmon

This sweet mustard takes only 20mins from pan to plate, making it a quick and easy meal to enjoy any time of the week.

Servings: 4

Total Time: 25mins

Ingredients:

- Nonstick cooking spray
- 4 (6 ounce) salmon fillets
- 2 tbsp freshly squeezed lemon juice
- 3 tbsp yellow mustard
- ¼ cup packed brown sugar

Directions:

1. Spritz a 15x10x1" baking pan with nonstick cooking spray.

2. Arrange the salmon on the baking pan.

3. Drizzle lemon juice all over the fish and lightly brush with yellow mustard.

4. Scatter brown sugar over the top and bake, uncovered until the fish flakes easily when using a fork, for 12-15 minutes.

5. Serve and enjoy.

Author's Afterthoughts

I would like to express my deepest thanks to you, the reader, for making this investment in one my books. I cherish the thought of bringing the love of cooking into your home.

With so much choice out there, I am grateful you decided to Purch this book and read it from beginning to end.

Please let me know by submitting an Amazon review if you enjoyed this book and found it contained valuable information to help you in your culinary endeavors. Please take a few minutes to express your opinion freely and honestly. This will help others make an informed decision on purchasing and provide me with valuable feedback.

Thank you for taking the time to review!

Christina Tosch

About the Author

Christina Tosch is a successful chef and renowned cookbook author from Long Grove, Illinois. She majored in Liberal Arts at Trinity International University and decided to pursue her passion of cooking when she applied to the world renowned Le Cordon Bleu culinary school in Paris, France. The school was lucky to recognize the immense talent of this chef and she excelled in her courses, particularly Haute Cuisine. This skill was recognized and rewarded by several highly regarded Chicago restaurants, where she was offered the prestigious position of head chef.

Christina and her family live in a spacious home in the Chicago area and she loves to grow her own vegetables and herbs in the garden she lovingly cultivates on her sprawling estate. Her and her husband have two beautiful children, 3 cats, 2 dogs and a parakeet they call Jasper. When Christina is not hard at work creating beautiful meals for Chicago's elite, she is hard at work writing engaging e-books of which she has sold over 1500.

Make sure to keep an eye out for her latest books that offer helpful tips, clear instructions and witty anecdotes that will bring a smile to your face as you read!

Made in United States
Orlando, FL
19 April 2022

16947299R00081